Manning Park

Lorraine Harris

DEDICATION

To my old friend
Bob Boyd
The Laird of Manning Park

ACKNOWLEDGEMENTS

R.H. "Bob" Boyd, First Forestry Park Ranger.

Wayne Stetski, Manager, Lower Mainland Regional Interpretation and Information Parks and Recreation Division.

Gail Ross, Manning Park. With grateful thanks for the use of her personal collection of pictures of Manning Park.

Manning Park

An All-Seasons Playground

Lorraine Harris

ISBN 0-88839-972-3
Copyright © 1984 Lorraine Harris

Catalog in Publication Data

Harris, Lorraine, 1912-
Manning Park

    Includes index.
    ISBN 0-88839-972-3

        1. Manning Provincial Park (B.C.) 2. Parks — British
Columbia. I. Title.
FC3815.M35H377   917.11'4   C83-0911626
F1089.M3H377

All rights reserved. No part of this publication may be reproduced, stored in a retrieval system, or transmitted, in any form or by any means, electronic, mechanical, photocopying, recording or otherwise, without the prior written permission of Hancock House Publishers.

Edited by Diana Ottosen
Typeset by Elizabeth Grant in Times Roman
  on an AM Varityper Comp/Edit
Layout by Dorothy Forbes

Printed in Canada by Friesen Printers

Published simultaneously in Canada and the United States by

HANCOCK HOUSE PUBLISHERS LTD.
19313 Zero Ave., Surrey, B.C. V3S 5J9
HANCOCK HOUSE PUBLISHERS INC.
1431 Harrison Avenue, Blaine, WA 98230

Table of Contents

Introduction 6
The Beginning 7
The First Trails 8
The Dewdney Trail — Royal Engineers Road 9
Survey for the Great Northern Railroad 12
Trappers 13
Wildlife 15
Mining 17
Logging 19
R.H. (Bob) Boyd, First Park Ranger 20
The Burn 24
Year-Round Playground 26
Alpine Meadows 29
Summer Recreation 30
Hiking 32
Winter Sports 35
Christmas at Pinewoods Lodge 40
Manning Park Lodge 40
Operation of the Park 41
Indian Names 42
Interesting Place Names 44
Index 47

The Three Brothers Mountains provide a challenging setting for backpackers. G. ROSS

Introduction

Manning Park, one of British Columbia's Provincial Parks, contains 176,000 acres (71,300 hectares) of mountains, valleys and magnificent scenery. It is essentially a mountain park with deep, narrow valleys and heavily forested mountains, with a good ski area and interesting trails to scenic plateaus, lakes and campsites. In winter it is a fairyland of giant mountains of pristine white dipping to snowcovered trenches torn by glassy frozen creeks. Its boundaries extend from the West Gate, 16 miles (26 km) from Hope, 37 miles (59 km) east to what used to be Tower's ranch; from the U.S. border to the headwaters of Whipsaw Creek, its northernmost extremity. This park is a public favorite because of its accessibility to Vancouver and the fact that the Hope-Princeton Highway passes through the middle of it. It offers a year-round playground to skiers, fishermen and campers.

The Beginning

In 1931 George Melrose, district forester, Kamloops Forest District, was travelling through the Three Brothers Plateau looking for open grazing land when he realized the potential of the area. The Three Brothers Mountain Reserve was formed to stop overgrazing of the alpine meadows by domestic sheep. By 1936 it was recognized by the population of Princeton that the area should be further protected and they assisted Melrose in bringing this to the attention of the government. As a result the Three Brothers Game Reserve was formed. By 1941, at the insistence of the Princeton Board of Trade, the Three Brothers Mountain Park was gazetted as a Class A Provincial Park to protect the alpine meadows and Lightning Lake area.

At this time a cairn was erected at Similkameen Falls in honor of Mr. E.C. Manning, the Provincial Chief Forester who had been killed in a plane accident. The Falls were then within the Park boundaries, and from there to the present eastern boundary there were many pieces of privately owned property. This was also the area where most of the mine-staking took place. The boundaries were then changed to accommodate the mining interests and the cairn was moved to its present location in front of the Headquarters buildings.

The Scenic Hope-Princeton Highway at the two-mile point.   G. ROSS

The First Trails

The Skyline II Trail provides backpackers with a first-hand look at Manning Park.

G. ROSS

The first travellers through what is now Manning Park were the coastal Indians who travelled over the present Skyline Trail to the Similkameen Valley where they hunted, fished and visited with the Similkameens. The Coast Salish first went into the mountains in search of berries and marmot. A peaceful way of life was established, the coastal people traded dried salmon and oolachans (candle fish) for wild hemp, fish nets, dried berries and ochre from Vermillion Forks, now Princeton. The red ochre was a prized commodity because the pigment, used for dye and paint, was not available on the coast. The trip from the coast usually took fifteen days.

The first white man to travel through this area was Alexander Ross, who arrived in January 1813. Ross was a clerk in a fur company. Archibald McDonald explored the area in 1827 and sketched an early map.

Further development came after the Oregon Treaty was signed and the U.S.-Canadian border was moved north from the Columbia River to the 49th parallel. This prevented the Hudson's Bay Company traders from using the Columbia River as a transportation route to the Pacific so Alexander Caulfield Anderson was commissioned by the Hudson's Bay Company to open up a new route through the Cascade Mountains. With Indian guides he opened up a fur brigade route from Hope to the Tulameen River.

The Dewdney Trail — Royal Engineers Road

The discovery of gold along the Similkameen and at Rock Creek in 1859 forced Governor Douglas to find a way to keep communications open to the mining camps and to keep the Americans from invading the goldfields and taking the wealth back across the border. In 1860 he sent Edgar Dewdney of the Royal Engineers to survey and build a pack trail on the Canadian side of the border. By 1861 the Royal Engineers had completed twenty-five miles of road from Hope. Disputes over tolls and more gold discoveries elsewhere caused work to cease. In 1918 after World War I, an influx of people caused road-building to start again, but it soon subsided. Road-building started in 1929 with the unemployed working on the road. Once again it was interrupted until the Second World War when the interned Japanese worked on the road for a short time. It was finally finished in 1945.

Today parts of the old Dewdney Trail are in evidence along the Hope-Princeton Highway as far as the Rhododendron Flats.

Park visitors get a spectacular view of the Hozameen Mountains from the Skyline I Trail.
G. ROSS

The Royal Engineers constructed many roads in British Columbia, including this portion of the Dewdney Trail.
J.E. UNDERHILL

Edgar Dewdney of the Royal Engineers
B.C. PROVINCIAL ARCHIVES

Where the trail was built by the Royal Engineers the grades were steep and the sides riprapped with rock walls.

Before the completion of the Hope-Princeton Highway on November 14th, 1949, three trails were used for passage through this mountain country: the Skyline Trail, the Allison Pass Trail and the Hope Pass Trail.

The Skyline Trail was used by the Indians for many years when they went to the mountains to hunt for marmot (commonly called the whistler). The soft furry hides were used for making sleeping robes. They also collected berries from the interior which they dried and brought back to the coast. Skyline Trail started at the confluence of the Skagit River and Ross Lake at the U.S. border, went up over the coastal mountains into the Lightning Lakes area and down to Princeton. It also went into the Flat Top Mountains and through the Ashnola Region.

Mount Hozameen towers over the Skyline Trail.   G. ROSS

The Allison Pass Trail followed the old wagon road built by the Royal Engineers in 1859 and 1860 to Skagit Bluffs, along nearly the same route as today's road. This trail and the pass are named for the government representative who was a pioneer in the Princeton area. The Allison Pass Trail was known as the lower road and always kept open as it was easier for winter travelling for the prospectors and trappers. It was gradually improved from the Princeton side into a wagon road and during the depression years of the 1930's relief camps were set up and the men completed a rough wagon road from Princeton to Allison Pass, at an altitude of 4,500 feet (1,372 m).

The Hope Pass Trail built by Captain Grant of the Royal Engineers was shorter and less hazardous than the Dewdney Trail. While the Dewdney Trail turned north at Snass Creek, the Hope Pass Trail continued east, turned north at the Skaist River, past the southern foot of Skaist Mountain, through Hope Pass and the upper portion of Whipsaw Creek, and on to Princeton.

A hiker stops to enjoy the view from the Blackwall meadows.

J.E. UNDERHILL

Survey for the Great Northern Railroad

At one time the engineers of the Great Northern Railroad and a reconnaisance crew went through the Three Brothers Plateau doing a survey to bring the Great Northern from the U.S. to a Canadian terminal at Keremeos and on to the coast. This route did not come to pass as it was preceded by the CPR's completion of the Coquihalla Railroad from Hope to Princeton, where it met the mainline from Spence's Bridge to Kamloops.

The engineers of the Great Northern were followed by developers who staked lots by the river at what is now known as Cambie Campsite. They staked much of the mountainside, as high as the 5,000 foot (1,524 m) level. There were some very large lots laid out in the area of the present ranger station and the stakes can still be found there. This development failed when the Great Northern did not build the railroad.

Trappers

After the goldrush, trappers and miners were in this area before it was gazetted for a park, and mining claims and traplines were prevalent. After the Park was created, mining, logging and trapping activities ceased within its boundaries. One trapline issued before the gazetting is still held by Joseph Hilton.

Paul Johnson, the first trapper in this area, trapped marten, mink and beaver in the 1890's. His cabin was built at the present damsite area. Johnson once killed 100 black bears in one season.

In 1904 Johnson sold his trapline to two brothers known as "the state of Mainers," because they were from the state of Maine in the United States. In 1904-1905 they took many pelts from this alpine plateau. In about 1908 they sold their interests to two brothers, Harry and Bill Gordon, who walked over the mountains from Hope and trapped wildlife in the Three Brothers Plateau area from 1908 to 1938. All of these trappers were headquarted at the confluence of the Chuwanton, Castle Creek and Similkameen rivers, at what is now Muledeer Campsite east of Manning Park Lodge, then called Poverty Flats because of the poor trapping. In 1938 Harry Gordon sold his trapping rights to Joe Hilton, who today lives in Princeton and has the only private occupancy rights in the Park.

Joe Hilton is responsible for supplying the Parks Branch with much information about names, places and events that occurred in the Manning Park area.

Joe Hilton had twenty cabins on his trapline, which covered 150 miles (240 km) of mountainous terrain. Some of these were just shelters consisting of a box about seven feet by three feet (2 by .9 meters) with just enough room for a bed, and a table on which to place a stove. In winter he travelled mostly on snowshoes, a slow mode of travel.

Joe Hilton trapped until the park was gazetted, after which he assisted Forest Ranger Bob Boyd, and was eventually hired by the ranger. The second year Boyd was in Manning Park he gathered boards from a relief camp and Joe Hilton helped him construct his first cabin. Both lived in the cabin for the summer. Joe worked on and off in the Park from 1946 to 1975.

All trappers and prospectors were very safety conscious and aware of the possibility of accidents, and when they went out for two or three months at a time they always let people know where they were going, identifying the areas precisely by name.

"Similkameen" stretched from Princeton to the junction of Pasayton. "Roach River" went from the Pasayton Roach cabin to three forks where the Chuwanten, Cambie and Castle Creeks joined it. From there it was "Cambie Creek" as far as Allison Pass, where the stream coming in from the north was called North Cambie and from the south was the Memaloose.

Black bears were once a common sight in the Park.　　　DAVID HANCOCK

Bob Boyd was responsible for introducing elk into Manning Park.
D.V. DAVIDSON

Wildlife

Wildlife in the park was once plentiful, and included black bear and grizzly, found mostly near the U.S. border.
Moose: first appeared in 1955 and increasing steadily.
Cougar: very scarce.
Mountain Beaver: rarely seen as they are nocturnal. These animals cut down lupines and hang them on low tree branches to dry.
Lynx: not plentiful.
Weasel: seen in large numbers.
Marten: this was known as "big marten country."
Wolverine: practically never seen.
Fisher: very rare.
Elk: introduced to the Princeton area in 1933, some later appeared in the Park.
Columbia Groundsquirrels: originally came from Penticton through the Osprey Lake area.
Flying squirrels: abundant but rarely seen as they are nocturnal.
Hoary Marmots: seen at Hansen Creek and Memaloose. The Indians hunted them for their pelts to make sleeping robes.

The Whiskey Jack, a friendly mountain bird. G. ROSS

Mule deer can be seen throughout Manning Park.   G. DEORKSON

Red and Douglas Squirrel hybrids: the hybrid has a creamy underside.
Wolves: not plentiful.
The population of all the above mentioned, except squirrels, has decreased, due to traffic, people and logging.

Hoary marmots make their home in Manning Park's subalpine meadows.

M. ROSS

Mining

Well known prospectors from the early days include Charlie Bonnevier, a Swede who immigrated to New York and worked his way west to Similkameen in about 1898-1899, where he settled and prospected. His territory was from Whipsaw Creek through the canyon to Big Muddy. He told Joe Hilton that he could make fifty dollars a day panning across from the railway station in Princeton. With this money he tunneled and mined in the Roach River country without much success. Bonnevier claimed it took four days on snow shoes to travel from Princeton to Manning, but an experienced, strong individual could make it in one long day. Other well-known prospectors were Broman, Jack Crowley, and Hughey Kennedy.

Mines such as Big Ben Mines, at the headwaters of the Similkameen, have never been operated as producing mines, but the claim has been improved each year and could be mined as it was staked before the park was gazetted. Essential development work was done on Bolivar, Canam and Robinson claims. All claims were proven and in good standing.

The Steamboat Mountain claim was made around 1900. Steamboat Mountain is on the west boundary of the Park, above and east of Skagit River approximately 6 miles (10 km) from where the Skagit enters Ross Lake. This claim produced very rich samples and caused quite a flurry on the Vancouver stock market. It created a scandal when it turned out to be a salted mine.

Mining claims in Manning Park, although not very lucrative, were promising enough to keep prospectors looking for the elusive gold. The Act which banned prospecting in the park aroused the anger of many, but only those claims which had been staked before gazetting could stand in good stead. However, none have been actively mined as no assessment nor active work can be done within the Park. Owners, however, may retain the rights to the claim.

Logging

Timber licences issued before the gazetting of the Park can still be held by the stakers. These licences were procured by staking one square mile of timber, surveying it, and registering it, for a small fee, with the Provincial Government. If ground rental was not paid, the licence had to be surrendered. No licences have been granted since the plateau was gazetted as a park.

Good timber tracts far back in the mountains were often discovered by prospectors, who would then sell this information to loggers or companies for about fifty cents an acre. Two logging operations, begun in this manner, have been allowed within the park boundaries over the years. Their operations have shut down and no others have started up in the Park. Hopefully this will remain so as logging would horribly scar the wilderness beauty.

The Park officially opened in November 1950, and was named after Ernest C. Manning in memory of the then recently deceased Provincial Chief Forester who had been killed in a plane crash. Although he was not the originator of the idea of using the land for a park, he was a keen conservationist. Many people, however, thought this park should have been named after George Melrose, who was the first to recognize the value of this alpine wilderness area.

But all in all, the dreams of everyone who planned this wilderness have now been realized with its development as an all-seasons playground.

← **Tall unbroken forests are found throughout the Park.**
G. ROSS

R.H. (Bob) Boyd, First Park Ranger

Prior to 1957 all provincial parks came under the jurisdiction of the Forest Service. The first park ranger at Manning Park was R.H. (Bob) Boyd. He went into the park to set up his headquarters at the present site of the Park offices, making the trip from Princeton in a model-A Ford. He traversed the area alone on foot and horseback the first year and planned many trails and camp areas. It is due to the foresight and dedication of Bob Boyd, the "Laird of Manning Park," that so many good trails, campsites and hiking areas are open today. He was the leading figure in planning what was then Pinewoods Lodge and the Park headquarters. The area's sites and buildings were designed in alpine style. The main objective was to transform the area into an alpine wilderness park where the public from both the coast and the interior could enjoy its grandeur and natural charm.

Bob Boyd came well equipped for the job of forest park ranger after serving twelve years in the B.C. Forest Service. He had been engaged in parks work for several years, opening parks on Vancouver Island, and constructing and planning their layout

The Three Brothers Mountains stand watch over the Heather Trail.
G. ROSS

with the assistance of the appointed forester. In 1937, for example, he opened the first trail from Stuie (Bella Coola) through the Rainbow Mountains into Tweedsmuir Park in preparation for Lord Tweedsmuir to make the trip. During the war years when all parks were closed he was engaged in forestry work. This, together with his work in the Port Alberni district, prepared him well for the 1946 appointment as a forest ranger in Manning Park. He spent 1946 to 1948 constructing trails, fighting fires, and doing general reconnaissance in the Park. He had the help of only two men in 1946-1947, one being Joe Hilton. The three built a barn for the saddle and pack horses they used to cover this rugged area. The structure still stands.

Between 1946 and 1949 reconnaissance work was carried out in order to implement the development of the park. Park development was already well underway when the Hope-Princeton Highway was opened in the fall of 1949. In 1948 contracts were let for the ranger station and Pinewoods buildings, the lodge and gas station. These were completed in the spring of 1950 and the park was officially opened in May 1950

with many of B.C.'s major forestry men attending.

One major achievement credited to Ranger Boyd was the changing of the Act governing prospecting in the parks. A man and his wife prospecting in the park attempted to stake claims in the Lightning Lakes area, one of the Park's main attractions. They were stopped by Boyd, who objected strenuously. Boyd realized the rules would have to be changed and brought the matter to the attention of Chief Forester C.D. Orchard, who took it up with the government. Subsequently the Act was changed, prohibiting prospecting and staking in any class "A" park.

The road to the Alpine Meadows was another Boyd project. He realized the value of constructing this road early in the park's development. He started to convert the existing trail into a road with help from the B.C. Telephone Company which needed access to their microwave tower on top of the mountain. Today this road is one of the main attractions during the month of August when the alpine flowers are blooming in profusion. Access trails wander through the meadows around the plateau.

The dam built at what was then Beaver Tree Lakes, a swamp

The Skagit River passes near the base of towering Steamboat (or Shawatum) Mountain. G. ROSS

Many visitors choose to stroll along the canyon's self-guiding trail. G. ROSS

area of beaver sloughs, created the Lightning Lakes. The cairn erected on this dam contains a piece of stone from Blarney Castle brought back from Ireland by Bob Boyd, who presided at the official opening.

Ranger Boyd was often called "The Laird of Manning Park" in recognition of the vital role he played in the life of the park. His men had a sign painted to this effect and hung in the dining hall of the ranger station.

Boyd retired after seventeen years of continuous service in Manning Park and twenty-nine years in the Forest Service. He was the last of the Forest Rangers to be in charge of a park. On his retirement the Parks Branch appointed a Park Supervisor resident at the station. Boyd's picture still hangs in the Headquarters office at Manning Park.

Boyd saw practically all the present major developments completed before his retirement. Some new campsites have since been added as well as improvements made to the ski areas, but he oversaw the development of the lodge, dining room, coffee shop, motels and stable for riding horses.

Ye Olde Manning Park Gallows were located at "The Burn" for many years.
B.C. PROVINCIAL ARCHIVES

New growth slowly covers the scars left after a forest fire raged through the Park.

The Burn

Manning Park's one scene of tragedy is camouflaged in winter by a soft mantle of snow and in summer nearly camouflaged by the new growth of naturally seeded forest. Not long ago this was a large tract of burned land through which the highway passed, an eyesore and constant reminder of the terrible toll taken on our forests and recreation areas by sheer carelessness.

This area known as "The Burn," was once as well forested as the rest of the Park, but in August 1945 before the road was completed from the west side, a giant fire was started and it burned out of control until extinguished by fall rains. It is presumed to have been started by two motorcyclists travelling over the old wagon trail, camping overnight in a surveyor's shake cabin and failing to put out their breakfast fire. Firefighters from Hope and Princeton could not contain the fire.

G. ROSS

On a carpet of green, the skeletons of burned trees stand, stark monuments to man's carelessness.
G. ROSS

Year-Round Playground

Manning Park with its 176,000 acres (71,300 hectares) of mountains, lakes and magnificent scenery, is a year-round playground for the Lower Mainland and Okanagan-Southern Cariboo regions. Situated an easy three-hour drive from Vancouver and less from the Kamloops-Okanagan area, the park spreads north and south of the Trans-Canada Highway (southern route), with year-round travel possible. A great variety of activities for hikers, campers, fishermen, skiers and all outdoor types is available within short distances of the area where Manning Park Lodge is situated.

Manning Park is well used by the public, from those seeking winter and summer recreation to those who come to the lodge for meals and a look at the superb scenery.

The serene Lightning Lakes are favorite destinations for campers. W. STETSKI

The scenic Hope-Princeton Highway at the two-mile point. G. ROSS

Alpine Meadows

The potential of the alpine meadows as a tourist attraction was recognized at an early stage in the Park's development. The trail to the meadows was developed into a blacktopped road for part of the way, with a good dirt road continuing up to the Lookout. Situated halfway to the top, the Lookout, complete with parking facilities, offers a breathtaking view of the valley below, including Manning Park Lodge, Frosty Mountain, Lightning Lakes as well as a splendid view to the east. The colorful carpet of alpine growth is a joy to the botanist and nature lover with its profusion of wild white and red heathers, many varieties of the daisy family, lilies, marsh marigolds, the ever plentiful lupines and many others. Hikers feel they've at last reached the great open spaces and are walking on top of the world when they breathe the crystal clear air of the alpine meadows and gaze at the magnificence of the unsurpassed vista of the Cascade Range.

Manning Park's beautiful subalpine meadows.   A. GRASS

← The view from Cascade Lookout.   G. ROSS

Manning Park annually plays host to thousands of campers.

B.C. PROVINCIAL PARKS

Summer Recreation

In summer the Park is as beautiful as in winter. The hillsides display all the colors of the spectrum. Nature's many shades of green are splashed together with the reds of Indian Paint Brush, vivid yellow wild buttercups, blue lupines and wild bluebells, while the sandy slopes offer orangey-yellow musk and the violet shades of the wild aubretia. All this scenery is easily accessible from a good highway running through the Park, bordered by rivers and streams full of small Rainbow, Cutthroat and Dolly Varden trout. Picnic sites complete with cedar tables and benches, are well-spaced and conveniently situated on the roadside. Camping areas under the supervision of the Parks and Outdoor Recreation Division guarantee clean and well planned campsites. Lightning Lakes picnic ground is one of the best situated for family use, with attractive playgrounds, and fishing, swimming, boating and hiking in the immediate surroundings. Some campsites have interesting names such as Muledeer, named for the member of the deer family that frequents the area. Muledeer campsite is situated about four miles (6.4 km) east of the Lodge. Coldspring, named for the spring of cold clear water in the camping ground, is about 1.25 miles (2 km) west of Manning Park Lodge and Hampton, named after Hampton Creek about three miles (5 km) east of Headquarters. These are strategically placed far enough off the highway to ensure privacy for campers. All individual sites contain a clean, cleared spot for a tent, trailer or camper, and a fire pit with chopped wood supplied by park employees. Water, tapped from the clear mountain streams, is readily available.

Park naturalists conduct nature walks in the morning during the summer, pointing out interesting flora and fauna. Afternoon walks take the tourist into the alpine meadows to discover the mountain flowering plants. Nature trails for those who wish to wander on their own are well marked with such attractive names as Paint Brush, Canyon and Beaver Pond.

A vista center situated by the Lodge parking lot, provides information on what to see and where to find it. The center provides pamphlets listing mountain flowers of many varieties; naming and describing many of the twenty-two kinds of butterflies recorded as residing in the Park. The many varieties of butterflies are attracted by the different climates in the Park: the moist west coast forest, dry interior, and alpine and sub-alpine areas. Each of these climates produce three distinct kinds of vegetation.

An interpretive walk in the subalpine meadows.   W. STETSKI

Hiking

Hiking trails guarantee an exhilarating walk and constantly entice the ardent hiker to take new trails. The Frosty Mountain Loop and Poland Lake Trail are just two of many trails. The former is a full day's hike and not to be undertaken by the "Sunday walker." The magnificence and grandeur of the Park's scenery accounts for the hiker's admiration of the Frosty Trail. It is a circular trail leaving the highway at the Pacific Crest Trailhead 1¾ miles (3 km) east of the Park Headquarters and heading south. Up the mountain the trail forks; one fork leads to Windy Joe Lookout on Windy Joe Mountain, an old forest fire lookout. The other fork goes on past Frosty Mountain, so named because of the everpresent snow. The trail comes down by the

Visitors to Manning Park can enjoy magnificent views of the subalpine meadows. G. ROSS

A tired hiker takes in the breathtaking view from the summit of Frosty Mountain. S. SHORT

Lightning Lakes and joins the road back to the Lodge completing a circle of fifteen miles (24 km).

The trail to Windy Joe is an old access road to the forest fire lookout. It is about an 8% grade and is kept cleared by the Park employees. It is planned that where once the old lookout was will become an interpretive site with information telling its past and present as well as identifying points of interest in the distance.

The Poland Lake Trail begins at Strawberry Flats and travels past the ski area at Gibson Pass and on to Poland Lake, a beautiful lake of clear green water nestled in a high alpine valley. The trail then drops to the headwaters of Memaloose Creek. This is a good walking trail of graduated slopes and is 10½ miles (17

The Windy Joe Fire Lookout provides fire rangers and visitors with an unobstructed view of the park. B.C. PROVINCIAL PARKS

km) of exciting scenery.

Other walking trails are Lightning Lakes Loop, Nepopekum Falls Trail, Pacific Crest Trail (Canadian portion), Skyline Trail, Chain Lakes Trail, and Heather Trail. All are interesting walks except Pacific Crest, which is essentially a tougher hiking trail.

Horseback riding is now restricted to designated horse trails: Hope Pass, Cathedral Provincial Park, Monument 83, Windy Joe, Pacific Crest and Dewdney.

The Lightning Lakes chain is an attraction for the keen fisherman and the canoeing enthusiast. Flash Lake, 1½ miles (2.4 km) long and 30 feet (9 m) deep, cannot be seen from the road and offers good fishing for rainbow trout. Boating is confined to rowboats and canoes in order to preserve the peace and solitude of the natural environment. There is a good road from Manning Park Lodge to the lakes. Boats are launched from this road to go to the Lightning Lakes chain to keep the shoreline free from launching areas and parking lots, which mar the natural beauty of the lake's surroundings.

The spectacular scenery from the Orange Chair.   B.C. PROVINCIAL PARKS

Winter Sports

Skiing is the main attraction in this winter wonderland, because snow conditions are excellent and usually last until late April. The Park's potential for a ski resort was first discovered when a group of men went in to survey the possibilities of winter recreation.

It was in February 1946, before the official opening of Manning Park, when Assistant Forester C.P. Lyons, Mount Seymour Forest Park Ranger Ole Johnson, and Vancouver's well known skier and jumper Tom Mobraaten, made a trip to Manning Park to assess the winter sports possibilities. They left from Princeton travelling over a one hundred mile (160 km) route, which took ten days. It was the first time the trip had been made on skis. Their assessments indicated great possibilities for various winter sports.

The first skiing in Manning Park took place in the winter of 1952-1953 close to the Park Headquarters on Sugar Loaf Hill. Although Sugar Loaf was too steep for a rope tow the con-

Cross-country skiing is one of the prime winter sports in Manning Park.
G. ROSS

struction of this tow was the first attempt to develop winter sports and year-round activity in Manning Park. The tow served for a year and a half when a better tow was installed in December of 1954. This served as transportation for hill skiing for four years, when Blackwall Road construction made finding a new location necessary. Just above the former Pinewoods service station, where the present road starts up to the alpine meadows, a new slope was cleared and in 1960 a Poma Lift was installed to provide a longer ski run.

Skiing at Manning assumed larger proportions in 1962 when the dream of hosting the Winter Olympics sent officials looking for suitable ski slopes. Gibson Pass was considered but eventually judged unsuitable and the project was dropped. However, the idea of developing Gibson Pass as a ski area remained alive. With the ever increasing effort to make Manning Park more accessible to the public, road construction to the Pass began in 1964. A survey to locate a ski hill took place, and in 1965 a clearing was made and a twin rope tow built. The Poma Lift was moved from Pinewoods and in 1966 was installed above the twin tow at the Pass. It did not work well and in 1967 was replaced by the Blue Chairlift. That year turned out to be a big one for skiing at Manning. The present beginner's hill was cleared and equipped with the rope tow from Pinewoods hill. In 1969 the T-Bar was placed below the rope tow, and in 1970 the Orange Chairlift came into service. In 1977 the twin rope tow was removed and intermediate slopes were cleared below the Blue Chairlift. Manning Park skiing soon became popular. In the early days accommodation was sometimes inadequate and hammocks were

Manning Park offers many opportunities for recreational development.
B.C. PROVINCIAL PARKS

Sunny weather and good snow conditions attract many cross-country skiers along Manning Park's Lightning Lake Chain. G. ROSS

slung in the lower quarters of the staff building of Pinewoods Lodge and rented at a very nominal fee. Although accommodation has been improved and the name changed to Manning Park Lodge, the ski area has not needed major changes except for improvements to the ski runs. Cross country skiing has become popular throughout the Park, and is suitable for people of all ages. There are 100 miles (160 km) of marked trails and 16 miles (26 km) of groomed cross country trails. Many older people have been introduced to the sport through the accessibility of the area and the ski lessons offered.

The coffee shop at Gibson Pass Day Lodge is open only in the winter for skiers and tourists. Practically all the slopes in the bowl-like Gibson Pass offer excellent skiing and are easily reached from the tows and chairs. Prices are fair and competitive with other resorts of this size.

T-Bar length — 427m (1,423 ft), capacity 650 per hour.
Rope tow length — 168m (560 ft), capacity 900 per hour.

Manning Park is a skier's haven during the winter. Ski runs such as the Blue Face offer skiers many challenges. G. ROSS

Some interesting facts about Gibson Pass are:—
• It is the same altitude, within just a few feet, of Allison Pass and the snow level at Gibson can be gauged by measuring snow at Allison and adding eight feet (2.4 meters).
• The Lodge is situated right where the Great Northern Railroad was proposed before the Coquihalla Railroad was built.
• There is skating behind the Lodge, tobogganing and sleigh riding.

A completely natural playground for children in the area of the Lodge makes the Park a winter attraction for the whole family. Christmas at Manning now has to be booked two years ahead of time to ensure oneself accommodation at the Manning Park Lodge.

Christmas at Pinewoods Lodge

Christmas at Pinewoods Lodge has been enjoyed by many city dwellers and in Boyd's time was booked for six months ahead by those seeking an old fashioned Christmas. The Park buildings were decorated with many colored lights and the high alpine architecture was outlined in color against winter's white mantle, creating a fairyland effect. The lodge catered to the guests by offering special holiday fare, a Christmas tree and decorations. "The Laird" always played Santa Claus. Those not lucky enough to obtain a cabin could book a hammock in the basement of the service lodge.

Manning Park Lodge

In 1971 the Commissionaire left Pinewoods, taking the name with him. The lodge complex was then taken over by Headquarters, operated by parks personnel, and renamed Manning Park Lodge.

The accommodation at the Lodge is more than adequate, offering attractive rooms at the motel as well as housekeeping cabins. There are thirty-three sleeping units, eight motel kitchen units, four triplex chalets, fifteen family cabins, restaurant, saunas, recreation room, ping pong and tennis courts. All this is in a magnificent setting, a valley set between high mountains and surrounded by forest and streams. The original hotel burned to the ground on November 11, 1970. This was rebuilt and Manning Park Lodge was officially opened in 1972 by W.A.C. Bennett, Premier of British Columbia.

The campgrounds in the headquarters area have a total of 353 sites. The wilderness campgrounds are a little further from the main lodge area and there are nine available to the public with cleared spaces in a completely natural setting.

Manning Park, which has developed from a wilderness game reserve to a great tourist attraction, has appeal for the city dweller and the outdoorsman alike. We in British Columbia are fortunate and owe a debt of gratitude to those who had the foresight to preserve it as a park, to those who developed it into a year-round playground and to those who will continue to look after it and add further attractions for future generations.

Operation of the Park

Gibson Pass Resort Incorporated took over the operation of Manning Park Lodge, Restaurant, Gibson Pass downhill and cross-country ski areas, and the canoe rental facilities on July 3, 1984.

Gibson Pass Resort Incorporated is composed of ten British Columbia businessmen who believe parks are for the use and enjoyment of all. They plan to operate the concessions and skiing facilities to best serve the public. The company has bought all the buildings with the exception of the Blackwall Camp area and has been given a fifty-year park-use permit to operate within the core area of Manning Park. Campgrounds and recreation areas are to be retained and serviced by the Parks Branch.

Mr. Roy Morrow of Hope is president, Mr. Al Priebe, also of Hope, is secretary-treasurer, and Mr. Mike Yakimovich of Chilliwack is vice-president. This new group plans to make some improvements to make Manning Park a year-round recreation area all British Columbians and tourists can continue to enjoy and be proud of.

The beautiful Personnel Building provides staff accommodation.   G. ROSS

Indian Names

(From *A History of Manning Park* by Al Grass, an unpublished report written for the Ministry of Lands, Parks and Housing).

Indian names often tell interesting stories about an area, J.N. Cameron calls them "reminder of their travels."

There are, however, a number of problems connected with the meanings of names:
(a) frequently they are loose phonetic interpretations of actual Indian names;
(b) there are local meanings of names which cannot be easily translated;
(c) a word can have several meanings depending upon the context and accompanying body language.

This wildflower called Indian Paintbrush splashes bright reds over Manning Park in the summer.   M. ROSS

Presented here are Indian names from the Manning Park area *for which meanings could be found.*
1. **SKAGIT** — refers to "a settlement of Indians on the Skagit River."
2. **SUMALLO** — means "upriver Indians."
3. **SNASS** — means "rain."
4. **SIMILKAMEEN** — also spelled **"TSEMEL-KA-MEN"**. **"SCHIM-ILICHAMEACH"**, **"SA-MILK-A-NEIGH"** and **"SIM-LKAMEUGH."** There has been a great deal of confusion over this name. The two commonly held meanings are "Valley of Eagles" and "Salmon River." The Similkameen Indians were sometimes referred to as the "Eagle People" because eagles used to be plentiful in the Similkameen Valley, and their tail feathers were an item of export.
5. **MEMALOOSE** — means "Dead Deer."
6. **NICOMEN** — "near a small creek."

Interesting Place Names

The serene beauty of a Manning Park lake.   G. ROSS

(From *A History of Manning Park* by Al Grass, an unpublished report written for the Ministry of Lands, Parks & Housing).

Place names have been selected on the basis of interesting background. There are others, of course, but it was felt that the following have a special significance in terms of the Park's history.

Allison Pass — named after J.F. Allison, a pioneer in the Princeton area. It was Allison who originally recommended the southern route for trappers and prospectors to Governor James Douglas (J. Walter).

Beaver Pond — originally known as "Dead Lake."

Blackwall Peak — originally known as "Haystack Mountain."

Boyd's Meadow — named after Robert Boyd, Manning's first "ranger." Boyd was appointed in 1946, after twelve years' service with the B.C. Forest Service. "So much a part of the work and life of the park was Ranger Boyd, he was often called, 'The Laird of Manning Park'." Boyd retired in 1963 after 17 years of continuous service in Manning Park and 29 years in the Forest Service.

Cambie Creek — upper reaches of the Similkameen; also a former campground. Possibly named after H.J. Cambie, who helped seek a route through the Cascades for the Canadian Pacific Railway.

Bonnevier Creek and Bonnevier Ridge — named after Charles Bonnevier who arrived in Princeton in 1804. Homesteaded near present East Gate. Operated the Red Star Mine for 23 years. Cleared 35 miles (56 km) of trail connecting with the Dewdney Trail.

Goodfellow Creek — named after the Rev. Goodfellow of Princeton.

Grainger Creek — named after M.A. Grainger of the Princeton Board of Trade. Grainger wrote a letter to the Commissioner of Grazing in 1929 in which he said there was sufficient grazing land elsewhere and that the "Hope-Summit County" should be saved for a park reserve.

Lightning Lakes — formerly known as the "Quartet Lakes."

McDiarmid Meadows — named after a pioneer family who settled in the East Gate area.

White-tailed ptarmigan camouflaged against a rock.   TOM W. HALL

Index

Accommodation, 40
Allison Pass, 44
   Trail, 10-11, 14, 39
Alpine Meadows, 7, 22, 29
Anderson, Alexander C., 8
Ashnola Region, 10
Bear, Black, 13, 15
   Grizzly, 15
Beaver, 13, 15
   Pond, 44
   Tree Lakes, 22
Bella Coola, 21
Bennett, W.A.C., 40
Big Ben Mines, 17
Big Muddy, 17
Blackwall Camp, 41
Blackwall Peak, 44
Blarney Castle, 23
Boating, 30, 34
Bonnevier, Charlie, 17, 45
Bonnevier Creek, 45
   Ridge, 45
Boyd, Robert H. (Bob), 13, 20, 23, 40, 45
Boyd's Meadow, 44
British Columbia Forest Service, 20
British Columbia Telephone Co., 22
Broman, 17
Burn, The, 24
Butterflies, 31
Cambie Creek, 14, 45
   Campsite, 12
Campsites, 12-13, 30-31, 40-41
Canadian Pacific Railway, 12
Canoe rental, 41
Cascade Lookout, 29
Cascade Mountains, 8, 29
Castle Creek, 13, 14
Chain Lakes Trail, 34
Christmas, 39-40
Chuwanton River, 13, 14
Coast Salish, 8
Coldspring Campsite, 30
Columbia River, 8
Coquihalla Railroad, 12, 39
Cougar, 15
Cross-country skiing, 38, 41
Crowley, Jack, 17
Dewdney, Edgar, 9
Dewdney Trail, 9, 11
Douglas, Governor James, 9
Elk, 15
Fish, 8, 30, 34
Fisher, 15
Flash Lake, 34
Flat Top Mountains, 10
Flowers, 22, 29-31
Forest fire, 24
Forty-ninth parallel, 8
Frosty Mountain, 29, 32
   Loop, 32
Gibson Pass, 33, 37-39, 41
   Day Lodge, 38
   Resort Incorporated, 41
Gold, 9, 17

Goodfellow Creek, 45
Gordon, Harry and Bill, 13
Grainger Creek, 45
Grant, Captain, 11
Great Northern Railroad, 12, 39
Hampton Creek Campsite, 30
Hansen Creek, 15, 30
Heather Trail, 34
Hiking, 30, 32-34
Hilton, Joseph, 13, 17, 21
Hope, 6, 8, 12-13, 24, 41
   Pass Trail, 10-11
   Princeton Highway, 6, 9-10, 21
Horseback riding, 23, 34
Hudson's Bay Company, 8
Indians, 8, 10, 15
Indian place names, 42-43
Ireland, 23
Japanese, 9
Johnson, Ole, 35
Johnson, Paul, 13
Kamloops, 7, 12, 26
Kennedy, Hughey, 17
Keremeos, 12
Lightning Lakes, 7, 10, 22-23, 29-30, 33-34, 45
   Loop, 34
Logging, 13, 16, 19
Lord Tweedsmuir Park, 21
Lynx, 15
Lyons, C.P., 35
McDiarmid Meadows, 45
McDonald, Archibald, 8
Maine, 13
Manning, Ernest C., 7, 19
Manning Park Lodge, 13, 26, 29, 40, 41
Marmot, 8, 10, 15
Marten, 13, 15
Melrose, George, 7, 19
Memaloose, 43
   Creek, 14, 15, 33
Mining, 7, 9, 13, 17
   Claims, 17
Mink, 13
Mobraaten, Tom, 35
Moose, 15
Morrow, Roy, 41
Muledeer Campsite, 13, 30
Nature Trails, 31
Nepopekum Falls Trail, 34
Nicomen, 43
Ochre, red, 8
Okanagan, 26
Oolachan, 8
Operation of the park, 41
Orchard, C.D., 22
Oregon Treaty, 8
Osprey Lake, 15
Pacific Crest Trailhead, 32, 34
Parks Branch, 13, 23, 41
Pasayton, 14
Penticton, 15
Pinewoods Lodge, 20-21, 38, 40
Poland Lake, 33

Poland Lake Trail, 32-33
Port Alberni, 21
Poverty Flats, 13
Priebe, Al, 41
Princeton, 8, 10-15, 17, 20, 24,
   Board of Trade, 7
Provincial government, 19
Rainbow Mountains, 21
Restaurant, 40, 41
Rhododendron Flats, 9
Roach River, 14, 17
Rock Creek, 9
Ross, Alexander, 8
Ross Lake, 10, 17
Royal Engineers, 9-10
   Road, 9, 11
Similkameen, 14, 17, 43
   Falls, 7
   River, 13
   Valley, 8
Skagit, 43
   Bluffs, 11
   River, 10-11, 17
Skaist
   Mountain, 11
   River, 11
Skiing, 35, 37-38, 41
Skyline Trail, 8, 10, 34
Snass, 43
   Creek, 11
Spences Bridge, 12
Squirrels, 15-16
Steamboat Mountain, 17
Strawberry Flats, 33
Sugar Loaf Hill, 35
Sumallo, 43
Swimming, 30
Three Brothers
   Game reserve, 7
   Mountain reserve, 7
   Plateau, 7, 12-13
Tolls, 9
Towers Ranch, 6
Trans Canada Highway, 26
Trappers, 13
Tulameen River, 8
United States Border, 6, 8-10, 15
Vancouver, 6, 17, 26
Vermilion Forks, 8
Wagon Road, 11
Weasle, 15
West Gate, 6
Whipsaw Creek, 6, 11, 17
Wildlife, 8, 10, 13, 15
Windy Joe
   Lookout, 32
   Mountain, 32
Winter Oympics, 37
Winter sports, 35, 37-9
Wolverine, 15
Wolves, 16
World War I, 9
World War II, 9
Yakimovich, Mike, 41

HISTORY TITLES BY HANCOCK HOUSE

Barkerville —
The Town That Gold Built
Lorraine Harris

Fraser Canyon —
From Cariboo Road to Super Highway
Lorraine Harris

Gold Along the Fraser
Lorraine Harris

Manning Park
Lorraine Harris

British Columbia Railway
Lorraine Harris

Walhachin —
Catastrophe or Camelot?
Joan Weir

Powell Lake
Carla Mobley

Gold Panning in British Columbia
N. L. Barlee

Gold Creeks and Ghost Towns
N. L. Barlee

Similkameen — The Gold and Ghost Towns of the Hope-Princeton Area
N. L. Barlee

Lost Mines — The Historic Treasures of British Columbia
N. L. Barlee

Gold! Gold!
Joseph Petralia

Backroad Adventures through Interior B.C.
Donovan Clemson

Old Wooden Buildings
Donovan Clemson

Living With Logs
Donovan Clemson

Craigmont Story
Murphy Shewchuk

Fur, Gold and Opals
Murphy Shewchuk

B.C. Recalled
Derek Pethick

Vancouver Recalled
Derek Pethick

Mighty Mackenzie
Lyn Hancock

Mackenzie Yesterday and Beyond
Alfred P. Aquilina

Fishing in B.C.
Forrester and Forrester

Mining in B.C.
G. W. Taylor

Trucking in B.C.
Andy Craig

Logging in B.C.
Ed Gould

Ranching in Western Canada
Ed Gould

Oil in Canada
Ed Gould

Big Timber, Big Man
Carol Lind

Nahanni
Dick Turner

Wings of the North
Dick Turner

Ralph Edwards of Lonesome Lake
Ed Gould

Ruffles in my Longjohns
Isabel Edwards

Fogswamp
Trudy Turner

Northern Man
Jim Martin

Novice in the North
Jim Robinson

Alaska Calls
Virginia Neely

Ho for the Klondike
G. Miller